Childhood in Wales

National Museum Wales Books

First published in 2010 by National Museum Wales Books, Cathays Park, Cardiff, CF10 3NP, Wales.

© the National Museum of Wales

ISBN 978 0 7200 0614 8

Text: Emma Lile, Gerallt Nash, Lisa Tallis
Design: Peter Gill & Associates
Editing: Mari Gordon

Welsh language edition available, *Plentyndod yng Nghymru*, ISBN 978 0 7200 0615 5.

All images are © the National Museum of Wales apart from the following: Darren Britton, p. 7; Brian Davies, p. 18; Eisteddfod Genedlaethol Cymru, p. 46; Frederic Evans, pp. 10/11, 17; T. Michael Evans, front cover; Nicola Leonard, p. 21, back cover; Simon Renault, p.38; Menna Roberts, p. 27; Beth Thomas, p. 24; Gwerfyl Thomas, p. 47; Raphael Tuck & Sons, p. 22; W. Williams, p. 15; John Williams-Davies, p. 3

Acknowledgements:
Emyr Davies, the late Mari Friend, Arwyn Lloyd Hughes, Lowri Jenkins, Brian Lile, Sue Renault, Miriam Rodrigues, Meinwen Ruddock-Jones, Megan De Silva.

This publication was prepared to coincide with the 'Childhood in Wales' exhibition at St Fagans: National History Museum, 7 December 2010 – 2 March 2011.

Cover image: David, John and Michael Evans with their uncle, Llangadog, 1930s.
Back cover image: Enjoying the sunshine in Pontcanna Fields, Cardiff, 2010.

Sponsored by
Welsh Assembly
Government

Contents

Introduction

Childhood, for many, signifies a magical time filled with fun and excitement, when friendships are forged and happy memories created. For others, the path to adulthood is difficult and painful, fraught with uncertainty, fear and worry. From sunny days and ice creams on the one hand to measles and bad school reports on the other, growing up will always have its joys and sorrows and countless challenges.

Whatever a child's background or circumstances, the power of play has spanned all generations, enabling children to escape into their own imaginary world and providing them with a sense of freedom and independence. From an early age, creative play teaches children to engage and interact with their own environment and helps them to develop physically, intellectually and emotionally.

Whereas children in Wales today generally enjoy plenty of leisure time, this has not always been the case. Until school attendance was made compulsory towards the end of the nineteenth century many young boys and girls were required to work in factories or mines, as poverty was rife and their earnings were needed to help keep their families clothed and fed. Life could be short. Fatal pit accidents were commonplace, while others suffered premature death because of poor hygiene and the lack of medicine and healthcare.

Page 3: Lift anyone?
Aberbanc, Ceredigion, early 1950s.
Right: Annie Evans with toy pram, Swansea, c. 1917.

The childhood collections at St Fagans: National History Museum are rich in artefacts, manuscripts, film and sound recordings, and provide a flavour of Welsh children's lives from the distant past to the present day. For all the profound changes in areas such as education, health and religion, the pleasures and pains, happiness and heartache of growing up are timeless and eternal.

Left: Little girl in her best dress, *c.* 1910.
Right: Fun on the slide, 2007.
Below: Making a splash, 21st century style.

Early years

The arrival of a baby into the world can be a time of great joy and excitement and, although most people remember little about their early years, a child's pre-school experiences can have a profound impact on later life.

Cradles and cots are possibly the most important pieces of furniture for a young child, and have long been used to establish a regular sleeping pattern. Tired and tightly swaddled, a crying baby can be lulled to sleep by a gentle swaying motion, much to the relief of frustrated parents.

Nursery rhymes, often set to song, have also been used for generations to settle or amuse babies and can forge a closeness between singer and child. There are many examples of Welsh counting rhymes using fingers and toes, which both entertain and educate by introducing new words and sounds.

During the sixteenth century the first high chairs were designed to be wedged against a table so that children could eat alongside their parents. The tray, or playboard, was added in the late nineteenth century, and provided more flexibility and comfort during mealtimes as the child could either use it as their own little table or as a space to put toys while being fed. As the high chair developed, many models could be transformed into different positions, from low chair, to chair with table or even a rocking chair! This multi-purpose approach continues today, and there are plenty of high chairs available that move up and down to effectively grow with the child.

Left: Small rocking chair with commode beneath seat, Glamorgan, *c.* 1730.
Below: Wooden cradle with a soothing blue interior, Cardiff, late 19th century.
Page 8: My first pose for the camera – John Evans, Swansea, 1939.

Pages 10/11: Children from Llangynwyd, Bridgend, *c.* 1905. Left: High chair made by David Nicol, 1889.

Perambulators, or prams as they are now known, are essentially vehicles in which babies can get out and about. Small carriage-type prams became popular in the nineteenth century, at a time when the benefits of fresh air were being actively promoted for all infants. Expensive and well made, they were initially status symbols for the wealthy and the middle classes, but became more affordable with the rise of mass production during the mid-twentieth century. Today we can get versatile all-in-one travel systems where a single product can be used as a pram, pushchair or car seat.

Osnath coach-style pram, Cardiff, 1960s.

Toys and games

Most of us can remember our favourite childhood toys and how they generated endless hours of pleasure and stimulation. Toys are not just a source of delight; they are also a vital part of learning and growing up, providing lasting comfort and enjoyment in a sometimes bewildering adult world.

Before the rise of mass-produced items during the twentieth century most children in rural Wales were proud owners of home-made toys and games constructed from whatever raw materials were available locally. Unsophisticated wooden objects such as whistles, spinning tops and rattles were commonplace, as were iron hooks and wheels and footballs made from pigs' bladders. Such traditional toys were usually made by parents or local craftspeople, and although generally simple in design they were invariably treasured possessions.

Above: A young sailor and his boat, Caernarfon, *c.* 1880.
Left: Julie Hughes and her favourite teddy, Porthmadog, *c.* 1951.

Before the mid-twentieth century few Welsh families had money to spend on anything apart from life's essentials, and this often meant creating one's own entertainment and amusement. Hours of fun could be had with games like hide-and-seek, hopscotch, making mud pies or hunting for flowers or butterflies. Young boys easily crafted paper kites, toy boats and catapults, while girls used their needlework ability to make rag dolls or play drapers' shops using scraps of material.

Above: A game of marbles at Llangynwyd, *c.* 1910.
Left: Playing cowboys, Carmarthen, *c.* 1910.

Whereas previously only wealthier parents could afford to buy toys for their children, the market was transformed with the growth of factory-made products during the post-war boom of the late 1940s and 1950s. The emergence of new, cheaper materials like plastic lowered prices and made toys available for children of all backgrounds. Renowned toy manufacturing companies, such as Mettoy, Wendy Boston and Louis Marx opened factories in south Wales and the branch of Lines Brothers, makers of Triang toys, at Merthyr Tydfil employed over a thousand staff at its peak. Mettoy

produced the Corgi range of toy cars at its plant in Swansea, including a model of James Bond's Aston Martin DB5, which remains the highest-selling toy car ever produced.

Page 18: Brian Davies on his Triang tractor, Llandygwydd, Ceredigion, *c.* 1966.
Below: Dalek, made by Louis Marx toy company, Swansea, 1960s.
James Bond Toyota GT, made in Swansea, *c.* 1967.

Above: Dolls house, Cardiff, *c.* 1903.
Right: Children playing on their
Nintendos, Penarth, 2010.

Toys are big business today and although most of those sold in Britain are made abroad, in recent years a growing number of home-grown products have appeared on the market. Figures created by Welsh animators for television such as Superted and Fireman Sam have generated attractive merchandise for children and have helped raise the profile of Wales both nationally and internationally. In recent years the power of television, film and advertising has meant that more and more toys are based on screen characters. Twenty-first-century

Wales, like Britain as a whole, is currently in the grip of a computer-games era, in which hi-tech entertainment is all-important. Perhaps rather surprisingly then, old favourites like Lego and Barbie dolls still have widespread appeal, and a continuing enthusiasm for perennials such as yo-yos, hula-hoops and skipping ropes proves that even the simplest of toys can, time and time again, delight succeeding generations of children.

Out and about

Up until the mid- to late nineteenth century many children were expected to work on farms, factories or underground in coal mines once they turned six or seven years of age. Even so, when they had some free time and gathered together on the street, in the fields or in the school yard they learned, played games and sang songs that were passed down from one generation to the next.

Increased leisure time during the twentieth century saw Sunday school trips and family holidays to the seaside or to the mountains of north Wales. The Scout and Guide movements and the Urdd (Welsh League of Youth) gave thousands of boys and girls their first experience of camping. Children from industrial areas would travel with their families, often by train, to spend a week or two at the seaside in places like Barry, Porthcawl and Aberafan in south Wales, or Llandudno, Prestatyn and Rhyl on the north Wales coast.

After the Second World War holiday camps such as Butlin's at Pwllheli and Barry Island, and Pontin's in Prestatyn, provided accommodation and organized entertainment for families and their children. Greater affluence and mobility have led to more adventurous holidays, although the simple delights of tents and caravans remain popular. Ironically, as foreign flights are cheap and easy to organize nowadays, many Welsh children have visited destinations such as Spain and Portugal but have never travelled around their own country.

We are enjoying Ourselves at COLWYN BAY.

Left: Fun at the seaside – a postcard
from 1914.
Above: Severn Road School football
team, Cardiff, season 1925-26.

Above: Little boy on his scooter, Llandovery, *c.* 1920.
Top left: Beth Thomas on her horse, Morriston, *c.* 1960.
Bottom left: Example of an early swing-boat, Carmarthen, *c.* 1910.

As to children creating their own entertainment at home, many older boys and girls continue to find a means of expression and independence with roller skates, bikes and skateboards.

Meeting up with friends at the local park or recreation ground can be just as enjoyable as going away on holiday.

Raleigh Chopper bike,
Swansea, 1970s.

Religion

Religion and the chapel used to be a key part of growing up in Wales, especially with the growth of Nonconformity during the nineteenth and early twentieth centuries. This encouraged regular attendance at the Sunday schools that had been established in chapels and churches across the country from the late eighteenth century. Reading the Bible at home was also important, and a child's familiarization with letters of the alphabet often came through biblical texts. During the evenings, or whenever there was a spare moment from the domestic routine, parents and grandparents often told Bible stories to the children or tested them with Welsh catechisms such as *Rhodd Mam i'w Phlant* (A Mother's Gift to her Children).

Above: Galltegfa Sunday School outing, Ruthin, early 20th century.
Below: Totally Teetotal! Band of Hope Certificate, 1882.

In addition to providing religious education for children of both rural and industrial communities, Sunday schools also offered varied leisure activities, such as days out, evening clubs and sports. For families unable to afford holidays, Sunday school outings were a real treat and the anticipation of a trip to the seaside for a swim and a picnic must have been immense. Singing in a choir, fancy dress competitions, village fêtes and plays were other forms of entertainment connected to the churches and chapels and a welcome relief from the hardships of normal daily life. Religious groups like the Band of Hope and Christian Endeavour gave children and teenagers the opportunity to socialize, while magazines like *Trysorfa y Plant* (The Children's Treasury) and *Seren yr Ysgol Sul* (The Sunday School Star) were published especially for children, with stories, poetry and competitions, as well as religious sermons and lessons.

With the growth of film, television and organized sport during the twentieth century, churches, chapels and their Sunday schools became less important to the everyday lives of children. However, even though fewer young people regularly attend a place of worship today, certain points in a child's life, such as birth and coming-of-age, continue to be celebrated in a Christian context. Christian families commemorate a baby's birth with a christening or baptism, and the white or ivory gowns usually worn are often treasured thereafter as a family keepsake. Similarly, the Jewish naming ceremonies, the Sikh teenage initiation celebrations and the Muslim feast to mark a child's birthday highlight the special place that continues to be held for boys and girls within other traditions.

Left above: Christening bowl, said to have been used in farmhouse services in Glamorgan, late 19th century.

Left below: Baptism in the river Ely, Cardiff, c. 1910.
Above: Toy model of Noah's Ark and animals, Cardiff, 1895.

When Jesus left his Father's Throne,
He chose a humble birth;
Like us unhonour'd and unknown,
He came to dwell on earth.

Sarah Williams Aged 14 Years 1833

Education

Formal education became a legal requirement in Britain in 1870, when an Act of Parliament stipulated that all children between the ages of five and thirteen should receive compulsory schooling. Before that, in Wales it was only the children of the wealthy or privileged who were educated, at the few private schools that were scattered around the country. Despite the widening of educational opportunities and the obligation to attend school, children in country areas were often absent at certain points in the agricultural year, such as sowing and harvesting, when their help was required on the farms.

Above: Collection of Welsh reading cards, 1927.
Left: Sampler, made by Sarah Williams, Llangynidr, Powys, 1833.

Unlike today, Welsh was seldom taught in schools. Indeed, during the early nineteenth century it was actively discouraged and pupils were punished for speaking the language, as it was feared that it would hinder their progress in English. The funding of schools was based largely on their performance in the so-called '3 Rs' – Reading, 'Riting and 'Rithmetic. The Welsh language owed its survival largely to the Sunday schools, where children and adults were taught to read and write in their own language, using the Bible as their textbook.

In 1914 the school-leaving age was raised to fourteen and certificates were awarded to children to confirm their suitability to begin paid work, meaning that the rest of their teenage years were spent acquiring vocational skills. A child's natural thirst for knowledge was aided during the late 1940s when, for the first time, radio and television programmes were made specifically

for a younger audience. Nowadays, children have their own dedicated television channels and the internet has transformed the ways in which they acquire information. Electronic data complements the printed word in the form of reference books and encyclopedias, and children can expand their education in the comfort of their own homes in whatever language or format they choose. This knowledge can be broadened further at eighteen years of age at one of Wales's numerous universities or colleges.

Left: Working hard at Maestir School, St. Fagans, 2009.
Above: Gardening lessons at Llangwm School, Denbighshire, c. 1920.
Pages 32/33: Penegoes National School, Montgomeryshire, 1905.
Pages 36/37: Botanical exercise book, Merthyr Tydfil, 1920.

Ecology of Order.

Few genera in this order are found wild in
Britain. In woods the Lily of the Valley is common
in some parts of England. Solomon Seal is also
found in woods, and in the upper part of shady
hedges. Wild Hyacinths and Garlic are also
found in woods.

-Butchers Broom is abundant in parts of
England. It is remarkable for its cladophyll
or modified stems.

The Wild Tulip, Yellow Star of Bethlehem,
Snake's Head occur in some parts of Britain.
The Herb Paris is found near streams local.
Bog Asphodel is found in marshes, and garlic
also favours shady riversides.

Many species are cultivated eg. Aspidistra
hyacinths and lilies for ornaments, the
onion, leek, Shallotte and chives, for domestic
purposes.

LILY OF THE VALLEY

TULIP

M CROCEUM.
ORANGE or SAFFRON
LILY!

Health

Historically, childhood in Wales could be a very dangerous time. During the nineteenth and early twentieth centuries overcrowding, lack of clean water and bad drainage made it easy for epidemic diseases like measles, scarlet fever and diphtheria to spread. Whooping cough was another serious illness, and caused nearly as many deaths as measles and smallpox combined. Many reformers thought ill health was an urban problem. In Merthyr Tydfil during the 1850s, for example, the mortality rate for children below one year of age was nearly 20 per cent. However, children living in the countryside also suffered ill health due to cramped housing conditions and poor diet. Inadequate nutrition

"Dont cry Mary, Mammy's got a bottle of MORRIS EVANS' OIL"
IN BOTTLES 1⁄3 & 3⁄-

Left: Playing nurse, late 1990s.
Above: Advertisement for Morris Evans children's medicine, 1930s.
Right: Young boys recovering from TB, Craig-y-Nos Sanatorium, Ystradgynlais, 1930s.

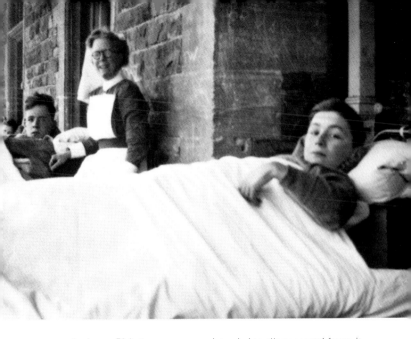

was a major issue. Rickets, a common complaint that led to bone malformation, was caused by a lack of vitamin D and was especially common in poor communities.

Owing to a lack of appropriate medicine and an effective vaccination system many illnesses were often fatal. Although the introduction of the Smallpox Vaccination Act of 1871 was intended to allay parents' fears, it aroused concerns for many because of horror stories in the press about healthy babies becoming fatally infected after receiving the vaccine. In Wales at this time calling the doctor out was simply too expensive and many people often turned to herbal and folk remedies to attempt to relieve suffering.

Despite outbreaks of serious illnesses such as cholera and tuberculosis, Public Health Acts in Wales during the late nineteenth century and better sanitation and healthcare services in the mid-twentieth century led to a great improvement in the nation's wellbeing. Issues surrounding nutrition and vaccinations continue today however, and government campaigns to encourage regular exercise and healthy eating among children are seen as essential in promoting all-round fitness.

Below: Pair of shoes belonging to a child who died aged seven months, Tonypandy, 1879.
Right: Baby weighing hammock, Rhondda, early 20th century.

ALL SAINTS CHURCH TREALAW

FIRMEES.1919.

Teenage years

When we think about childhood it is easy to forget about older children and teenagers. Yet these years are perhaps the most important, when childhood merges into adulthood and children gain their first glimpses and experiences of the wider world. For many this once meant hard work and increased responsibility on the farm, in industry, in the home or in service. Some respite was provided by Sunday school outings and Band of Hope meetings, while the local cinema and dances were also popular with teenagers as places to make new friends.

Teenagers at their confirmation, Trealaw, Rhondda, 1919.

The increasing affluence and social mobility of the 1950s and 1960s meant that more children had money for hobbies such as stamp collecting, chess clubs and going to dances and the cinema. Teenagers started spending more time at home in their bedrooms with friends listening to the latest pop records.

Above: Brian Lile's stamp album, Swansea, 1953.
Right: Victorian scrapbook, Pembrokeshire, 1880s.

Romance was also sought. From parading through towns and villages hoping to catch someone's eye during rituals such as 'Bunny Runs' and 'Monkey Parades', to dance dates and discos, courting was always an important milestone, especially if you 'clicked' with the person you liked. But in the past it was not all fun. With no sex education and limited methods of birth control, relationships could have serious consequences that affected the whole family. Today, alcohol, drugs and teenage pregnancies are emotive issues to be handled carefully and with sensitivity.

Teenage years can be exciting and trying in equal measure. Growing older is a difficult business: the later school years can bring the pressure of examinations, and the first days at university or work can be daunting. However, the thrill of new experiences and the culmination of childhood mark a break with the past, and can often bring a sense of heady expectation as we look forward to the next stage in life.

Left: Enjoying the National Eisteddfod at Bala, 2009.
Top right: Camping in the garden, Bridgend, 1979.
Right: Brothers on their bikes, 1977.

Wales's national museums

Amgueddfa Cymru is a family of seven museums located throughout Wales. Each family member gives a unique experience of Wales's history, while sharing the Amgueddfa Cymru values of excellence and learning.

The National Wool Museum
Dre-fach Felindre, Carmarthenshire

The National Waterfront Museum
Maritime Quarter, Swansea

National Museum Cardiff
Cathays Park, Cardiff

St Fagans: National History Museum
St Fagans, Cardiff

Big Pit: National Coal Museum
Blaenafon, Torfaen

The National Slate Museum
Llanberis, Gwynedd

The National Roman Legion Museum
Caerleon, Newport

More information can be found on the Amgueddfa Cymru website
www.museumwales.ac.uk